D1401960

SPACECRAFT

by Ruth Owen

PowerKiDS
press

New York

Published in 2015 by **The Rosen Publishing Group, Inc.**
29 East 21st Street, New York, NY 10010

Library of Congress Cataloging-in-Publication Data
Owen, Ruth.
Spacecraft / by Ruth Owen.
p. cm. — (Objects in space)
Includes index.
ISBN 978-1-4777-5875-5 (pbk.)
ISBN 978-1-4777-5879-3 (6-pack)
ISBN 978-1-4777-5877-9 (library binding)
1 . Space vehicles — Juvenile literature. I. Owen, Ruth, 1967-. II. Title.
TL793 O94 2015
629.47—d23

Produced for Rosen by Ruby Tuesday Books Ltd
Editor for Ruby Tuesday Books Ltd: Mark J. Sachner
US Editor: Sara Antill
Designer: Emma Randall
Consultant: Kevin Yates, Fellow of the Royal Astronomical Society

Photo Credits:
Cover, 1, 4–5, 7 (top), 11, 13, 15, 17, 19, 21, 23, 25, 27 © NASA; 7 (bottom)
© Shutterstock; 9 (top), 9 (center), 29 © Public Domain; 9 (bottom)
© Science Photo Library.

Manufactured in the United States of America
CPSIA Compliance Information: Batch # CW15PK: For Further Information contact
Rosen Publishing, New York, New York at 1-800-237-9932

CONTENTS

HUMAN SPACEFLIGHT

For more than 50 years, scientists and **engineers** from around the world have been designing, building, and sending spacecraft, **probes**, **satellites**, and other objects into space.

The spacecraft featured in this book have all carried humans into space. Humans have **orbited** Earth, traveled to space stations, and flown to the Moon. Sometime in the next 20 years, it is hoped that a spacecraft will carry astronauts to Mars.

Human spaceflight has been managed by government-run agencies such as **NASA** in the United States and the European Space Agency (ESA). In the future, spaceflight may become a **commercial** operation. This means that companies run by business people could plan and manage future missions to space.

Throughout the decades, some brave astronauts have lost their lives. The majority of human spaceflights, however, have been successful. Spaceflight is

The space shuttle *Atlantis*, on the launchpad at the Kennedy Space Center in Florida. It is being prepared for the 135th and final mission of NASA's Space Shuttle program. *Atlantis* flew this mission in July 2011.

extraordinarily dangerous, and so much can go wrong. The fact that so often it has gone right, however, shows the huge skills of the men and women who design, build, and fly spacecraft.

SPACE OBJECTS FACT FILE

In many ways, sending a robotic probe on a mission is easier than sending a spacecraft with a crew. Spacecraft that carry astronauts must be designed to supply oxygen. They must also carry essential supplies such as water and food.

On April 12, 1961, **cosmonaut Yuri Gagarin became** the first human to leave Earth's **atmosphere** and fly in space. This historic feat was achieved in a spacecraft named *Vostok 1*.

Vostok 1 was a spacecraft in the **Soviet Union**'s Vostok space program. It was designed to carry just one person.

Vostok 1 consisted of a ball-shaped crew capsule and descent module with a diameter of 7.5 feet (2.3 m). The capsule was nicknamed *Sharik*, which means "little sphere" in Russian. It was attached to the instrument module that contained most of the equipment and instruments needed to power and control the craft.

Gagarin did not fly *Vostok 1*. The spacecraft was controlled partly by automatic systems and partly by its mission control team on Earth. This was because scientists could not be sure how Gagarin would function in space and how his body would react to weightlessness.

SPACE OBJECTS FACT FILE

Vostok 1 had small portholes through which Gagarin could view the Earth. This was the first time a human had ever seen our planet from afar!

An instrument panel inside *Vostok 1*.

This 3D illustration shows how *Vostok* 1 would have looked in space.

Antennae kept *Vostok 1* in touch with Earth.

Entry hatch

Instrument module

Crew capsule and descent module

VOSTOK 1'S MISSION

Vostok 1 was launched into space aboard a Vostok-K rocket. It took off from the Baikonur Cosmodrome in the region of the Soviet Union that is today the independent country of Kazakhstan.

Once in space, Vostok 1 went into orbit. The spacecraft made one orbit of Earth. Then, small rockets on the craft, called retrorockets, fired up and positioned the spacecraft for its re-entry into Earth's atmosphere. As the spacecraft headed back to Earth, the instrument module and spherical descent module, or crew capsule, separated.

At around 23,000 feet (7,000 m) above Earth's surface, the capsule's entry hatch was released. Strapped into his seat, Gagarin was ejected from Vostok 1. His parachute opened, he detached from his seat, and floated safely back down to Earth. The capsule also parachuted safely back to Earth.

From launch to landing, Vostok 1's mission lasted 108 minutes. Sending a human safely into space was a huge technical achievement. The history of human spaceflight had begun!

SPACE OBJECTS FACT FILE

It was not possible to control Vostok 1's orientation as it re-entered Earth's atmosphere and experienced the scorching heat of re-entry. Therefore, the whole spherical capsule was encased in protective materials to create a **heat shield**.

Vostok 1 is launched into space aboard a Vostok-K rocket.

Yuri Gagarin aboard *Vostok 1*. As he blasted into space, Gagarin said "Poyekhali" to the scientists in mission control. It means, "Let's go!"

Vostok 1 back on Earth. The opened entry hatch and parachute can be seen on the right.

PROJECT MERCURY

On May 5, 1961, less than one month after Gagarin's historic spaceflight, a *Mercury* spacecraft carried the first American, astronaut Alan Shepard, into space.

Project Mercury was the United States' first human spaceflight program. The *Mercury* spacecraft, or capsule, was cone-shaped. On its wide, curved end it had a heat shield to protect the craft during re-entry to Earth's atmosphere. The single astronaut sat with his back to the heat shield in a seat that was made to mold perfectly to his body. After re-entry, the capsule, with the astronaut still inside, was designed to float back to Earth on a parachute and splash down in the ocean.

NASA built 20 *Mercury* capsules. They were used in test missions and in the eventual six missions that carried astronauts into space.

Alan Shepard did not orbit Earth, but traveled about 116 miles (187 km) above Earth's surface, and then returned. The entire flight lasted for just over 15 minutes. During his 1962 *Mercury* mission, astronaut John Glenn became the first American to orbit Earth.

SPACE OBJECTS FACT FILE

There were seven *Mercury* astronauts. They each named their capsule with the number 7. Shepard's spacecraft was named *Freedom* 7. John Glenn named his craft *Friendship* 7.

NASA technicians building a *Mercury* capsule.

The recovery compartment contained the spacecraft's parachutes.

Crew capsule

Heat shield

The *Faith 7 Mercury* capsule on display at Space Center Houston.

Alan Shepard aboard the *Mercury* spacecraft *Freedom 7*.

THE GEMINI PROGRAM

The Mercury program proved that NASA could safely send humans into space. Its Gemini program would take human spaceflight even further in readiness for missions to the Moon.

In order to reach the Moon, astronauts would have to spend many days in space. NASA would need to learn how to connect two spacecraft together while they were in flight. And a landing on the Moon would require astronauts to leave the safety of their spacecraft.

During 1965 and 1966, 10 manned and two unmanned *Gemini* missions were flown. The cone-shaped *Gemini* spacecraft were slightly larger than the *Mercury* capsule and held a crew of two astronauts.

During the *Gemini 4* mission, astronaut Ed White made the first-ever U.S. spacewalk, spending 20 minutes outside of his spacecraft. The *Gemini 7* crew stayed in space for two weeks. *Gemini 10* showed it was possible to join two spacecraft while in flight when it connected to the unmanned *Agena Target Vehicle (ATV)*.

The Gemini program proved that NASA had the technology to send humans to the Moon.

SPACE OBJECTS FACT FILE

The *Gemini 6* and *Gemini 7* spacecraft orbited Earth at the same time and met each other in space. *Gemini 6* was maneuvered to within 12 inches (30 cm) of *Gemini 7*.

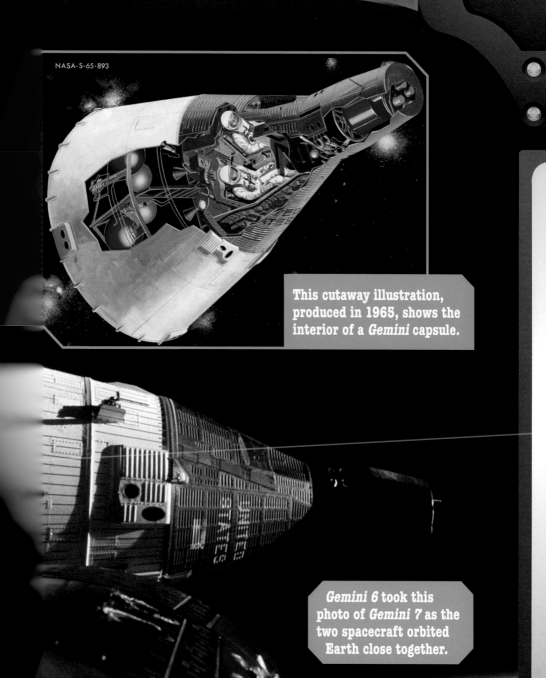

NASA-S-65-893

This cutaway illustration, produced in 1965, shows the interior of a *Gemini* capsule.

Gemini 6 took this photo of *Gemini 7* as the two spacecraft orbited Earth close together.

THE *APOLLO* SPACECRAFT

In the 1960s and early 1970s, NASA's *Apollo* missions carried astronauts to the Moon for the first time.

The *Apollo* spacecraft that made this possible were the Command Module (CM) and the Lunar Module (LM). The CM was the control center and living quarters for the three members of the crew. It contained the astronauts' seats, the control and instrument panel, the communications systems, and the heat shield and parachutes for the return to Earth. Attached to the CM was a Service Module (SM). The SM contained the craft's engine, fuel, and equipment to supply the astronauts with oxygen and water. Together, the CM and SM were called the CSM.

The Lunar Module was a lander that could carry two astronauts down to the Moon's surface.

The Moon missions were launched on Saturn V rockets. Once outside of Earth's atmosphere and on the way to the Moon, the Command/Service Module separated from the Lunar Module. Then the CSM turned around in space and docked, or reconnected, with the LM so that the crew's command module and the LM were joined.

SPACE OBJECTS FACT FILE

Once connected in space, the hatches between the Command/Service Module (CSM) and the Lunar Module (LM) could be opened. The crew could move from one spacecraft to the other and prepare the LM for its descent to the Moon.

If something went wrong during a take-off, the Launch Escape System (LES) could blast the Command Module (CM) and crew away from danger.

The Apollo 11 mission blasts off on July 16, 1969.

Command Module (CM)

Service Module (SM)

The Lunar Module (LM) is in here, encased in a protective aluminum structure.

This illustration shows an *Apollo* spacecraft approaching the Moon.

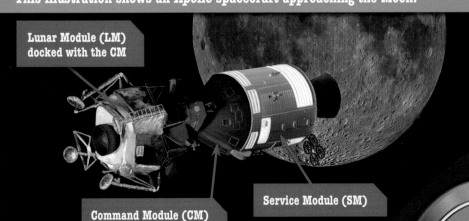

Lunar Module (LM) docked with the CM

Command Module (CM)

Service Module (SM)

LANDING ON THE MOON

The Apollo program included many missions. These ranged from test flights and unmanned missions to those that carried astronauts to the Moon.

The most famous mission is Apollo 11, when astronauts first landed on the Moon. The Apollo 11 Command Module (CM) was named *Columbia*. The Lunar Module (LM) was named *Eagle*.

On July 20, 1969, astronauts Neil Armstrong and Buzz Aldrin landed on the Moon's surface in *Eagle*. The LM's descent was controlled by computer, with Armstrong taking the controls for the final 2,000 feet (610 m). The third member of the Apollo 11 crew, Michael Collins, continued to orbit the Moon in *Columbia* as Armstrong and Aldrin made history by walking on the Moon!

A Lunar Module carried equipment for exploring the Moon's surface. It held a TV camera for sending images and movies back to Earth, tools for digging, and boxes to hold samples of Moon rock. On Apollo missions 15, 16, and 17, the LM carried a four-wheeled lunar rover, called the Lunar Roving Vehicle (LRV), or "Moon buggy." The rover allowed the astronauts to travel and explore far from their lander.

SPACE OBJECTS FACT FILE

On the ladder of each Apollo Lunar Module (LM) was a container holding a United States flag for the astronauts to place on the Moon.

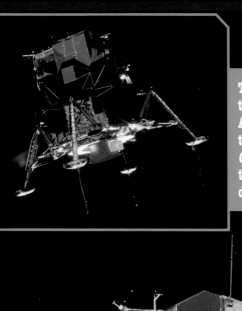

This photo of the LM *Eagle* was taken by Collins. Armstrong and Aldrin are inside. Collins had to check *Eagle* by looking out of *Columbia*'s windows to ensure the LM was in good shape for its descent to the Moon.

Buzz Aldrin unpacking experiments from the Lunar Module (LM) *Eagle* on the surface of the Moon.

BACK TO EARTH WITH *APOLLO*

When their time on the Moon was over, Armstrong and Aldrin took off in the top part of *Eagle*, the ascent stage. The descent stage, or bottom section, was used as a launch platform and is still on the Moon today.

Once up in space and orbiting the Moon, *Eagle* docked with the Command Module (CM), *Columbia*, and the astronauts climbed back into *Columbia*. *Eagle* was then jettisoned into space and eventually crashed back onto the Moon. *Columbia* then headed home.

Each Apollo crew used their Lunar Module (LM) in the same way and made their journey back to Earth in their CM. Just before re-entering Earth's atmosphere, the Service Module (SM) was jettisoned. The CM's heat shield protected the craft during re-entry. Then the CM floated back to Earth on parachutes, splashing down in the ocean.

SPACE OBJECTS FACT FILE

During the Apollo program, six missions landed astronauts on the Moon and brought them safely home. It was a phenomenal technical achievement not only for the brave astronauts but for the more than 300,000 scientists and engineers who contributed to the program.

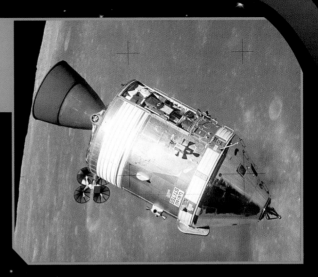

The Apollo 15 Command/ Service Module (CSM) orbiting the Moon, as viewed from the mission's Lunar Module (LM).

The Apollo 11 Command Module (CM), *Columbia*, floats in the ocean. The three astronauts and a Navy diver wait to be picked up by the aircraft carrier USS *Hornet*.

THE SPACE SHUTTLE PROGRAM

Many different spacecraft have traveled into space. These craft were designed to be used only once. On their return to Earth they were damaged beyond repair and could not be used again.

In its Space Shuttle program, NASA designed and built the world's first reusable spacecraft. Technically called the Orbiter Vehicle (OV), the craft is best known simply as the space shuttle. Six space shuttles were built. They were named *Enterprise*, *Columbia*, *Challenger*, *Discovery*, *Atlantis*, and *Endeavour*. *Enterprise* was a test craft, and was only used for test flights and landings.

Like earlier spacecraft, a space shuttle was launched into space by rockets. When its mission was complete, however, it could be flown back into Earth's atmosphere and, like a glider plane, landed on Earth, ready to be used again.

The Space Shuttle program flew missions for 30 years. The first mission, STS-1, was flown in the space shuttle *Columbia* in April 1981. Its two crew members were in space for two days and orbited Earth 37 times. In July 2011, *Atlantis* delivered a **payload** of supplies and equipment to the International Space Station (ISS) on mission STS-135. It was the final space shuttle mission.

Between them, the space shuttles flew 133 successful missions. Tragically, two missions ended in disaster. The space shuttle *Challenger* broke apart shortly after take-off in January 1986. In February 2003, *Columbia* broke apart as it returned to Earth. In each accident, all crew members aboard were killed.

Columbia lifts off to begin the first-ever space shuttle mission on April 12, 1981.

Atlantis prepares to dock with the International Space Station on the last-ever space shuttle mission. Its payload of supplies (the silver cylinder) can be seen in its cargo bay.

THE SHUTTLE

The space shuttles were the size of small airliners. Each shuttle could carry a crew of up to eight astronauts.

Inside each space shuttle there was a cargo bay and a crew cabin on three levels. The top level contained the flight deck and seats for four astronauts. The middle level contained more seats, the sleeping compartment, the galley, or kitchen, and the air lock. Wearing their spacesuits, astronauts entered the air lock before exiting the shuttle during space walks. The bottom level of the crew cabin held oxygen, water tanks, and equipment to remove poisonous carbon dioxide from the cabin's air.

To protect the shuttle from extreme heat or cold in space, and the intense heat of re-entry, each shuttle was covered with more than 24,000 protective tiles made from silica.

Just like a plane, a space shuttle had landing gear. As it approached the runway on return to Earth, three pairs of wheels were lowered from the shuttle's undercarriage.

SPACE OBJECTS FACT FILE

The space shuttles were 122 feet (37 m) long. From wing tip to wing tip, they measured 78 feet (23.8 m). A shuttle traveled at a top speed of 17,500 miles per hour (28,200 km/h).

This image was created by NASA to show the design of the cockpit on later shuttle flights. The seats are not installed in the picture.

Atlantis (mission STS-122) prepares to touch down at the Kennedy Space Center.

Some of the tiles that form a space shuttle's heat shield can be seen here on the underside of *Discovery's* wing.

THREE DECADES OF ACHIEVEMENT

The space shuttles acted as space laboratories, carried telescopes and other satellites into space, and helped build the International Space Station (ISS).

In April 1990, *Discovery* delivered the Hubble Space Telescope to its orbit around Earth. In 1993, *Endeavour* flew a mission to repair the famous telescope because its vision was blurred. *Endeavour's* Commander Dick Covey maneuvered the shuttle to within 30 feet (9 m) of the telescope. Then the telescope was captured by the shuttle's robot arm. As the shuttle orbited Earth for nearly 11 days, the crew made five spacewalks to carry out repairs.

Today, we're used to seeing incredible photos of the ISS in orbit. There was a time, however, when it was just a single module, named *Zarya*, launched by a Russian rocket. In December 1998, *Endeavour* carried the second module, *Unity*, into space and made the first connection between two ISS units. The shuttles continued to carry modules and parts to the ISS, and once the station was complete, they delivered supplies and flew ISS crews to and from the station.

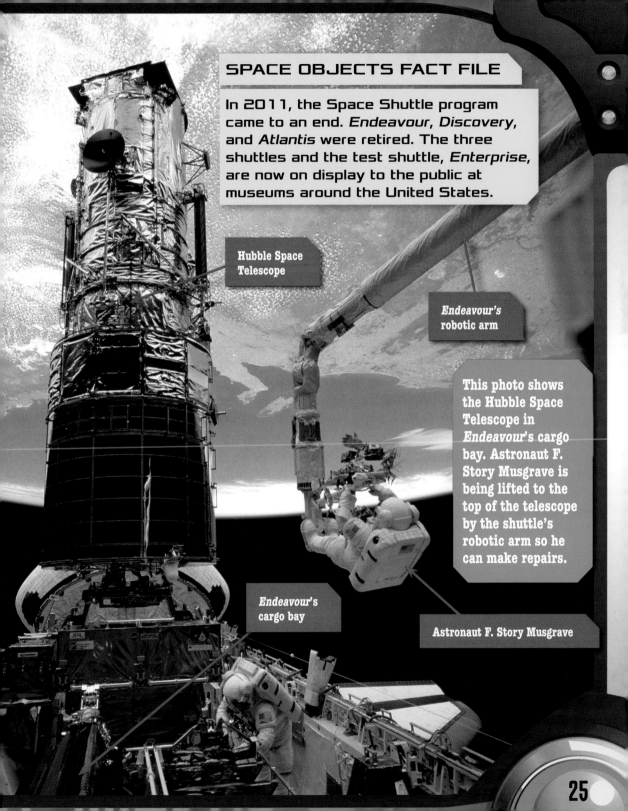

SPACE OBJECTS FACT FILE

In 2011, the Space Shuttle program came to an end. *Endeavour*, *Discovery*, and *Atlantis* were retired. The three shuttles and the test shuttle, *Enterprise*, are now on display to the public at museums around the United States.

Hubble Space Telescope

Endeavour's robotic arm

This photo shows the Hubble Space Telescope in *Endeavour's* cargo bay. Astronaut F. Story Musgrave is being lifted to the top of the telescope by the shuttle's robotic arm so he can make repairs.

Endeavour's cargo bay

Astronaut F. Story Musgrave

SOYUZ SPACECRAFT

Since the 1960s, the Soviet Union and now Russia have been sending humans into space aboard *Soyuz* spacecraft.

Today, the latest *Soyuz* spacecraft carry astronauts to and from the International Space Station (ISS). They also deliver food and other supplies. *Soyuz* spacecraft are launched on a *Soyuz* rocket from Kazakhstan.

A *Soyuz* spacecraft is made up of three modules. The orbital module is where the three-person crew lives when the craft is on a mission that requires it to spend time in orbit around Earth. The descent module is the section where the crew sits during launch, flights, and landings. The service module holds the craft's instruments, engines, batteries, and other equipment.

A *Soyuz* spacecraft takes six hours to reach the ISS. Its return journey takes just three and a half hours. A *Soyuz* does not splash down in the ocean or land on a runway. As it approaches the ground, it fires rockets and uses parachutes to slow down its descent. Then it hits the ground hard for a very bumpy landing.

SPACE OBJECTS FACT FILE

Like a ship's lifeboat, one *Soyuz* remains docked with the ISS at all times. If there's an emergency on the space station, the crew can use the *Soyuz* to escape back to Earth.

This photo shows two *Soyuz* spacecraft docked with the International Space Station (ISS).

Service module

Descent module

The orbital module is about the size of an SUV.

International Space Station (ISS)

TOMORROW'S SPACECRAFT

What types of spacecraft will be flying 10, 20, or 30 years from now? What missions will they fly?

Certainly, flights to the International Space Station (ISS) will continue. Perhaps, humans will return to the Moon, and one day, missions to Mars may begin. In the future, it's likely that many different spacecraft, built by companies as well as governments, will be heading for space.

The U.S. company SpaceX has developed the *Dragon* spacecraft. In 2012, *Dragon* became the first commercial spacecraft to carry cargo to the ISS. *Dragon* also has the capacity to safely bring large quantities of cargo from the ISS back to Earth. The *Soyuz* spacecraft cannot do this.

In the future, the *Dragon V2* spacecraft may carry astronauts to the ISS or even to another world. *Dragon V2* is designed to touch down on the surface of a planet as precisely as a helicopter. Then it can fly back to Earth, land, and be ready to fly again in a very fast turnaround time.

SPACE OBJECTS FACT FILE

Someday soon, it will be possible for any person—with enough money—to buy a ticket on a spacecraft and fly out of Earth's atmosphere as a space tourist.

The seven seats inside the crew compartment of *Dragon V2.*

The *Dragon* spacecraft approaches the International Space Station (ISS).

GLOSSARY

atmosphere
(AT-muh-sfeer) The layer of gases surrounding a planet, moon, or star.

commercial
(cuh-MUR-shul) Done by a business in order to make money.

cosmonaut
(KAHZ-muh-nawt) An astronaut from Russia, and before 1991 from the Soviet Union.

engineers
(en-jun-NIHRZ) People who use math, science, and technology to design and build machines such as cars and spacecraft. Some engineers design and build structures such as skyscrapers and bridges.

heat shield
(HEET SHEELD) An outer layer of a spacecraft, or section of a spacecraft, made from or covered with materials that protect the craft from heat and cold in space, and the intense heat of re-entry into Earth's atmosphere.

NASA
(NAS-ah) The National Aeronautics and Space Administration, an agency in the United States that studies space and builds spacecraft.

orbited
(OR-bih-tid) Moved, or traveled, around another object in a curved path.

payload

(PAY-lohd) The items carried by a plane or spacecraft. Payload can refer to cargo, such as food or scientific equipment, or crew members. In the case of the space shuttle, its payload could also be telescopes, satellites, and space probes.

probes

(PROHBZ) Spacecraft that study planets, moons, and regions in space. Probes do not have any people aboard and are remotely controlled by scientists on Earth.

satellites

(SA-tih-lytz) Objects that orbit another body in space, such as a planet. A satellite may be naturally occurring, such as a moon, or an artificial satellite used for transmitting television or cell phone signals.

Soviet Union

(SOH-vee-et YOON-yun) A former nation made up of a group of republics in parts of Europe and Asia. The Soviet Union broke up in 1991, creating a group of independent nations, including Russia, Ukraine, Kazakhstan, and Georgia.

WEBSITES

Due to the changing nature of Internet links, PowerKids Press has developed an online list of websites related to the subject of this book. This site is updated regularly. Please use this link to access the list: www.powerkidslinks.com/ois/craft

READ MORE

Holden, Henry M. *Danger in Space: Surviving the Apollo 13 Disaster*. New York: Enslow, 2013.

Omoth, Tyler. *Building a Spacecraft*. North Mankato, MN: Capstone Press, 2014.

Waxman, Laura Hamliton. *Exploring Space Travel*. Minneapolis, MN: Lerner Publications, 2013.

INDEX